LIVING
IN
DESERTS

LIVING IN DESERTS

A CULTURAL GEOGRAPHY

BY NAYANA CURRIMBHOY

FRANKLIN WATTS|1987
NEW YORK|LONDON|TORONTO|SYDNEY
A GROLIER COMPANY

"Life in Jigalong" on pages 54–58 has been adapted from *The Jigalong Mob: Aboriginal Victors of the Desert Crusade* by Robert Tonkinson. Copyright © 1974 Cummings Publishing Company, Inc. Used by permission of The Benjamin/Cummings Publishing Company.

On page 51, from W. H. Douglas, "The Desert Experience," in *Aborigines of the West* by Ronald M. and Catherine H. Berndt, eds. Nedlands: University of Western Australia Press, 1979. Used by permission.

Maps by Vantage Art, Inc.

Cover photographs courtesy of William Hamilton/Shostal Associates (top left); Irving Rosen/Shostal Associates (top right); © J. Ianiszewski/Art Resource, New York (bottom left); © Carol Beckwith (bottom right).

Photographs courtesy of © Georg Gerster/Photo Researchers: pp. 22, 66, 77, 84; United Nations Photo/John Isaac: pp. 23 (#153709), 24 (#153653); © Carol Beckwith: pp. 25, 28, 30, 31, 33, 37, 40; © Bernard Pierre Wolff/Photo Researchers: p. 26; United Nations/Gamma: p. 34; AP/Wide World: p. 47; Australian Information Service: pp. 48, 49, 53, 59, 60; © Diane Rawson/Photo Researchers: p. 51; © Omikron/Photo Researchers: p. 52; © Hubertus Kanus/Photo Researchers: p. 55; © Yvonne Freund/Photo Researchers: p. 61; © Victor Englebert/Photo Researchers: p. 67; Jack Ceitelis/Carfo: p. 70; © Carl Frank/Photo Researchers: p. 71; © H.W. Silvester/Photo Researchers: pp. 73, 74; Art Resource, New York: p. 78.

Library of Congress Cataloging-in-Publication Data

Currimbhoy, Nayana.
Living in deserts.

(A Cultural geography)
Bibliography: p.
Includes index.
Summary: Describes how the climate and resources of deserts affect the lives of people in Africa's Sahel, Australia's Western Desert, and Chile's Norte Grande.
1. Anthropo-geography—Arid regions—Juvenile literature. 2. Deserts—Juvenile literature. 3. Arid regions—Social life and customs—Juvenile literature. 4. Arid regions—Description and travel—Juvenile literature. [1. Anthropo-geography—Arid regions. 2. Arid regions. 3. Deserts] I. Title. II. Series.
GF55.C87   1987   304.2'0915'4   85-26597
ISBN 0-531-10145-2

CONTENTS

CHAPTER 1
AN INTRODUCTION TO DESERTS
11

CHAPTER 2
AFRICA'S SAHEL—
A HARSH LAND
19

CHAPTER 3
AUSTRALIA'S WESTERN DESERT
43

CHAPTER 4
NORTE GRANDE—
THE CHILEAN DESERT
63

CHAPTER 5
A COMPARISON OF
THREE DESERT REGIONS
81

GLOSSARY
87

FOR FURTHER READING
89

INDEX
91

To living in Shangri-la

LIVING
IN
DESERTS

1

AN INTRODUCTION TO DESERTS

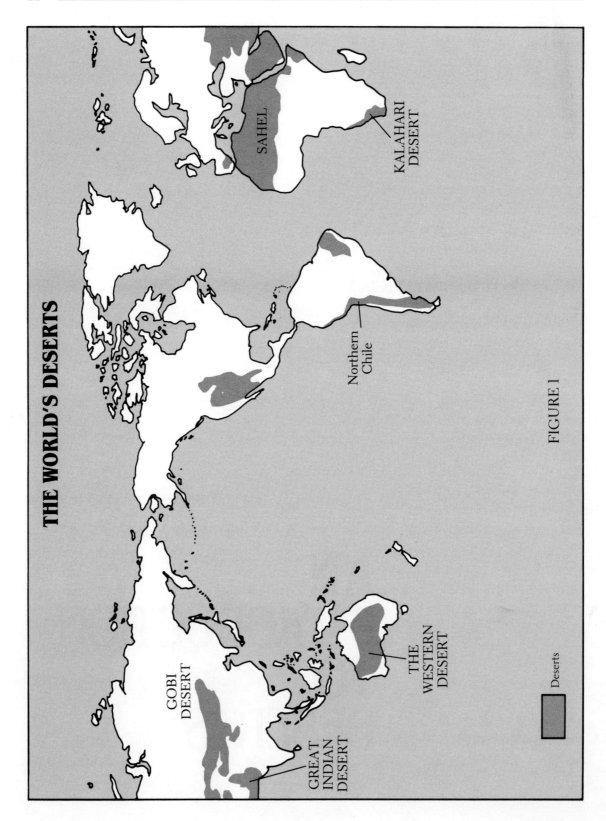

THE WORLD'S DESERTS

SAHEL

KALAHARI
DESERT

Northern
Chile

GOBI
DESERT

GREAT
INDIAN
DESERT

THE
WESTERN
DESERT

Deserts

FIGURE 1

Picture yourself sitting on the ground with your back to a hot wind that blows for weeks without let-up. You are drinking tea with your father and uncle while your mother and sister gather brush to fuel the evening fire. Though it is the end of the day, and the air is beginning to cool, it is well above 100 degrees Fahrenheit (37° C). You have just walked 10 miles (16 km) behind the family's cattle, keeping them in order. And in several weeks, when the meager pasture near this place is depleted, you will walk again until a new pasture is found.

Close your eyes and the scene changes. You are standing in a dry stream bed. On one side of the stream there is a school, a small clinic, and several small houses all made of cinder block. On the other side of the creek bed there is a haphazard collection of houses. Each house is built of canvas, poles, and tin sheeting. There is the smell of meat cooking on an open fire. The sound of a shortwave radio and a four-wheel-drive vehicle can be heard in the distance.

Close your eyes once again and imagine another scene. You are standing on the edge of one of the world's largest open pit copper mines. Enormous machines, mechanical shovels, and trucks are hauling millions of pounds of rock. Yet these machines, at the center of the pit, look small. They are more than five miles (8 km) away. It is not oppressively hot, the high temperature today was 80 degrees Fahrenheit (26° C). Miners, finishing their shift, are walking or taking buses home.

You have just been to a Wodaabe settlement in Africa's Sahel region, Jigalong in the Western Desert of Australia, and Chuquicamata in Chile. These three places are part of the world's desert region.

All the world's deserts have certain things in common. These include:

A *dry climate and sparse vegetation*— Deserts may be hot, such as the Western Desert in Australia, or they can be cold, but all deserts are dry. These arid lands receive less than 10 inches (25 centimeters) of rain each year.

Seasonal rainfall—There is a distinct dry season, with little or no rain. There is also a wet season during which most of the year's *precipitation* falls.

Low availability of water—Since there is so little precipitation, desert life and culture revolves around conserving and importing water. In traditional cultures, clothing has evolved to maintain comfort and retain as much of the body's water as possible. Where there is economic development in the desert region, water must be brought in by pipeline or truck at great expense.

Low population density—The world's deserts have low human population densities. This means they have very few people in comparison to regions with a wetter climate. Groups of people living in the deserts are often nomadic, moving from place to place to gain access to water, pasture, or food. Other desert residents are found living close to water such as rivers or natural springs.

Transportation problems—Because there are so few people, a lot of human time and effort is spent on travel between settlements. In each desert region, the overland journey to a larger settlement is a social event as well as an economic necessity. Goods that must come from outside the desert are often expensive, due to this long overland shipment.

Drought as a natural hazard—Rainfall in the deserts is not the same from year to year. There may be several wetter-than-average years in a row. Then several very dry years may follow, and human disaster can be the result, as cattle die and crops wither. Because there is so little rainfall, even a slight decrease may have very serious consequences.

Dependence on world systems—Even if desert settlements are remote and isolated, they are still tied to worldwide economic systems. For example, if the price of copper rises in New York City, the miners in Chile will be able to work longer hours and earn more money. If the price of copper falls on the world market, miners in Chile are laid off. If there is a drought in the Sahel and the drought lasts many years, people from around the world will be called upon to donate food and money to keep the people in this region from starvation. Economic and climate patterns tie deserts and human beings together around the world.

This book will compare and contrast the cultural geography of life in three different desert communities. In addition to learning about the desert communities, you will learn about the art and science of geography. You will also learn how cultural geographers study regions and how they view the relationship between people and their natural environment.

WHAT IS CULTURAL GEOGRAPHY?

Cultural geographers study the interwoven lives of people and their environments. Cultural geographers ask such questions as: How did the people who live here get here? How did they decide where to settle and how to make a living? How have they influenced their environment (land and climate) and how has it affected them? A major focus of cultural geography is how *culture* and *environment* fit together. By environment we mean the physical features of the world around us: the air, water, plant life, soils, and rocks that make up the world's biosphere. The biosphere is the envelope of life surrounding the globe. Culture is a way of life devised by human beings for getting along with the environment and each other. It is made up of beliefs, knowledge, religion, technology, economy, art, science, medicine, and philosophy. These are just a few of the elements of a culture. People around the world have put these elements together in different ways to create many different cultures.

In this book you will see that Wodaabe, Australian Aborigines, and Chileans have created very different cultures. Each culture is suited for the desert environment, but each uses the environment in a different way.

HOW CULTURAL GEOGRAPHERS STUDY REGIONS

A *region* is an area within which elements of culture or environment are similar. Outside the region, the elements are different. For example, if farmers in a certain area all grow the same crop, then you can draw a line around that area on a map and call it a region. Actually, though, regions are more complicated. A region is usually made up of several elements that overlap unevenly. For example, look at Figure 2 on page 16. It is a map of the world in which rainfall and vegetation patterns overlap. It separates the world into regions based on rainfall and vegetation.

Geographers can use information to map regions around the globe—on a world scale. Or they can look for more detailed regions at the scale of the nation. For example, the United States is separated into the Northeast, the Middle Atlantic, the Deep South, the Middle West, the Gulf States, the Southwest, and other regions, based on both objective and subjective information. Geographers gather objective information by observing and counting. This kind of information can include: rainfall, religion, settlement patterns, and vegetation. Geographers gather subjective information by carefully noting what people say and do in their daily lives or by listening to or reading the stories people tell one another. Subjective information tells geographers what region people believe they live in and how these people think their region is different from surrounding places. For example, in the United States, a woman might say she is a Southerner because she has spent an important part of her life, her childhood, for example, in the South.

The three desert communities described in this book are examples of *core areas*. These are areas where many objective and subjective elements of culture and environment overlap. As you move away from the core of a region, there will be fewer similar elements. As this happens, the region will gradually become more like the areas it borders. Often it is hard to decide what are the boundaries, or edges, of a region. For example, if you move north across the Sahel, there is less rain, less vegetation, and fewer settlements. As you move south from the Great North desert in Chile there is more rain, more settlements, and the most important way of making a living is by farming, rather than by mining. You are moving out of one region and into another. The boundaries between regions are not sharp, they are very gradual.

The more information used to define a region, the smaller the region is likely to be. For example, the world can be divided into big regions based on rainfall. But just imagine how many tiny regions you would have if, on top of rainfall, you laid down patterns of vegetation, religion, popular sports, and favorite desserts! Cultural geographers must decide what information to use when defining a region. They must also decide how much of this information must overlap to include a place within a region.

Figure 3 is a *model*. A model is a simplification of the real thing. In this case it is a simplification of a region. Figure 3 shows how objective and subjective

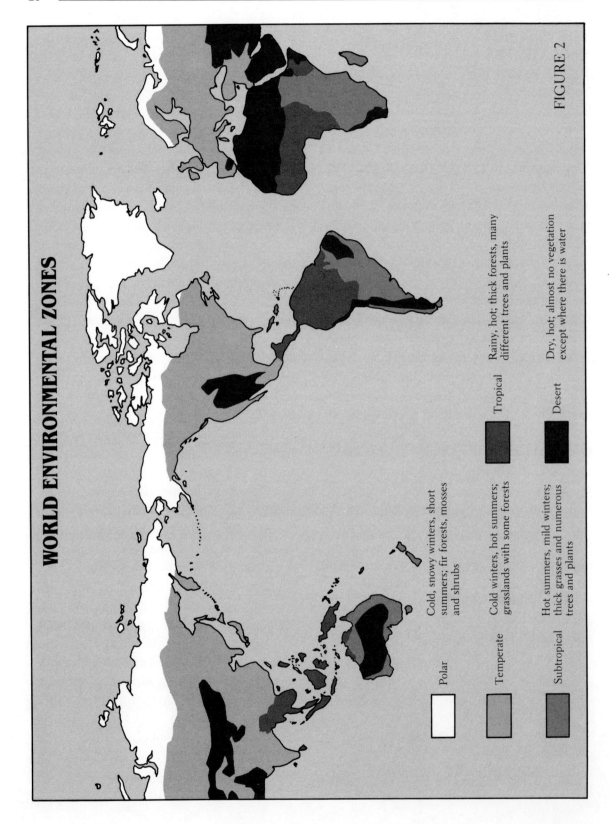

WORLD ENVIRONMENTAL ZONES

Polar — Cold, snowy winters, short summers; fir forests, mosses and shrubs

Temperate — Cold winters, hot summers; grasslands with some forests

Subtropical — Hot summers, mild winters; thick grasses and numerous trees and plants

Tropical — Rainy, hot; thick forests, many different trees and plants

Desert — Dry, hot; almost no vegetation except where there is water

FIGURE 2

A MODEL OF A REGION

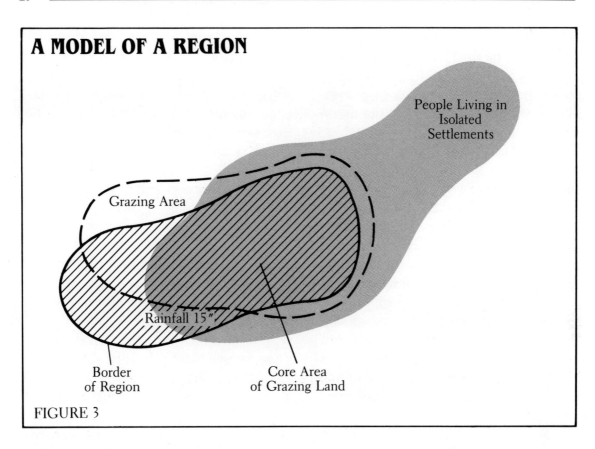

People Living in
Isolated
Settlements

Grazing Area

Rainfall 15"

Border
of Region

Core Area
of Grazing Land

FIGURE 3

information overlap to form a region, and how the core area gets smaller as more measures are added.

HOW ENVIRONMENT
AND CULTURE
FIT TOGETHER

You may be asking yourself how environment and culture fit together in the world's desert region. First, the environment does not determine the type of culture in a region. That is, rainfall and vegetation do not completely dictate how human beings use deserts. If people were only controlled by their environment, then all people in

all deserts around the world would be leading the same lives. But this is not so. Human choices and decision-making are not solely at the mercy of the environment. However, neither does culture completely control the environment. If people completely controlled the deserts, then all people in all the deserts around the world might be leading very different lives. But this is not so, because we have seen that there are many similarities among desert communities in the ways people adapt to the lack of water.

Culture and environment interact. That is, each one influences the other. For example, in Chile, the environment does not provide enough rainfall to raise vegetables. This means that the environment influences culture by limiting what can be grown. But, then, farmers may use irrigation or greenhouses to provide the necessary extra moisture for growing vegetables. If enough farmers use irrigation, they may use so much water that there will not be enough for other needs. Then water would become more costly in the future, since it would have to come from deeper wells or from farther away. In this case, human culture can influence the environment by determining how much water will be available in the long run. It may appear that culture has conquered the environment. But natural hazards such as drought can quickly overcome many improvements and changes. Recent severe droughts in the Sahel show us how drought and famine can easily affect large world regions.

Some cultural geographers believe that the more a culture uses its natural resources, the greater the risk of natural disaster. For example, the large families and many cattle of the Wodaabe allow these people a source of labor and a diet rich in dairy protein in years of plentiful rain. During these good years, Wodaabe women can sell dairy products, such as soured milk, for pins and eyelets used to decorate ceremonial clothing. When rain does not come, however, the Wodaabe suffer greatly. Cattle die of starvation and thirst. And people die of starvation. Many Wodaabe are forced to forgo their nomadic culture. This suffering is due to the lack of rain and the too-intense use of the Sahel to raise many cattle and to support large families.

When studying the world's desert region, cultural geographers may ask the following questions:

- How have culture and the environment interacted in this region?
- How do people, as children, learn to use their environment?
- If culture or the environment changes, will these people be able to keep up with the changes?
- How many families can the environment support?
- If the culture changes, can the environment support more or fewer families?
- How do people protect themselves from natural hazards such as drought?
- How successful or costly are their hazard protection methods?

As you study the world's deserts you can ask similar questions. These questions can also help you learn more about the region in which you live.

2

AFRICA'S SAHEL

A HARSH LAND

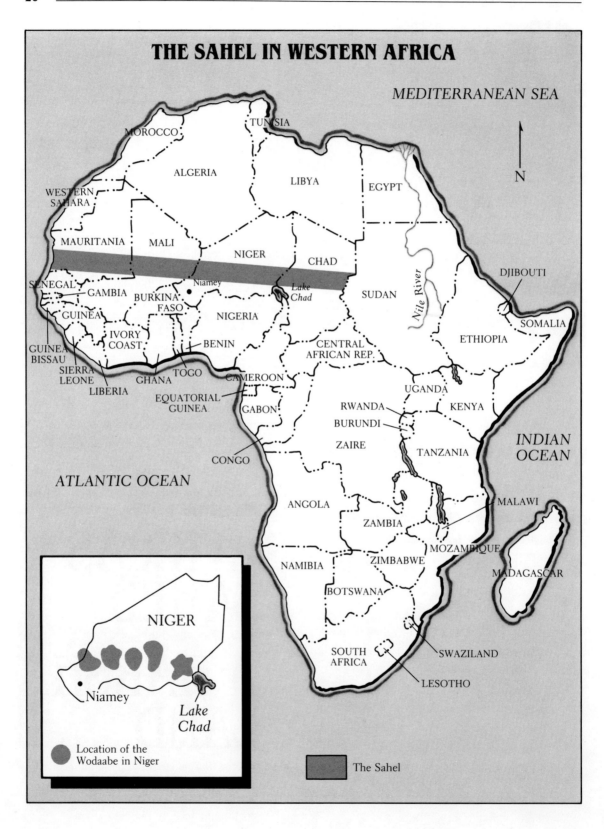

THE SAHEL IN WESTERN AFRICA

MEDITERRANEAN SEA

N

MOROCCO TUNISIA

ALGERIA LIBYA EGYPT

WESTERN SAHARA

MAURITANIA MALI NIGER CHAD

SENEGAL
GAMBIA BURKINA FASO Niamey Lake Chad SUDAN DJIBOUTI

GUINEA NIGERIA SOMALIA

GUINEA BISSAU IVORY COAST BENIN CENTRAL AFRICAN REP. ETHIOPIA

SIERRA LEONE GHANA TOGO CAMEROON

LIBERIA EQUATORIAL GUINEA GABON UGANDA

CONGO RWANDA KENYA

BURUNDI

ZAIRE

ATLANTIC OCEAN TANZANIA INDIAN OCEAN

ANGOLA MALAWI

ZAMBIA

MOZAMBIQUE

NAMIBIA ZIMBABWE MADAGASCAR

BOTSWANA

SOUTH AFRICA SWAZILAND

LESOTHO

Nile River

NIGER

Niamey

Lake Chad

Location of the Wodaabe in Niger

The Sahel

In Africa, between the great Sahara Desert and the grasslands of the south, lies an immense level plain. This area is a semi-desert land, scattered with scrawny bushes and stunted trees. Known as the *Sahel*—an Arabic word meaning "border"—the land runs through the six West African nations of Mauritania, Senegal, Mali, Bourkina Faso (once known as Upper Volta), Niger, and Chad.

The Sahel is a harsh land. It is a stark, sandy plain that stretches over 2 million square miles (518,000 sq km). Distances in the Sahel are great, and transportation is difficult. Few hard-top roads or railroads run across this vast, featureless expanse. The population, too, is sparse. There are only twelve people per square mile (five per sq km). Most of them live in the cities or along the banks of the Niger River.

In the Sahel, there is no rain for nine months of the year. During this time, the water in the wells is low, the pastures dry up, and the entire land lies brown and bare. The days are hot, and the nights sometimes freezing cold. To add to the discomfort, the searing desert wind, the *harmattan*, blows relentlessly. It throws sand into one's eyes and nose and clouds the air with a sandy haze.

The rains, which are often preceded by violent thunderstorms, fall between July and September. In this season, ponds and wells fill up, and the entire country-side turns a vibrant green. A peculiar characteristic of the Sahel, however, is that the rain cycles are unpredictable. So, al-though the average rainfall of the region varies from 4 inches (10 cm) in the north to 20 inches (50 cm) in the south, there are years when there is almost no rain.

This happened from 1967 to 1974. Over 300,000 people died before the rains returned to the Sahel. The region barely had time to recover from the tragedy when drought struck once again. Since 1982, the Sahel has been facing a famine that is even more devastating than the earlier one. In areas of Mauritania and Mali, for example, it has not rained at all for two years. Throughout the region, crops have failed, herds of cattle, sheep, and other animals have died, and millions of people are facing hunger and malnutrition. Even after the rains do fall, it will take a long time for the Sahel to return to normal.

PEOPLE OF THE SAHEL

The Sahel is the home of the Wodaabe, a slender, bronze-skinned people with delicate features. The Wodaabe are *nomads*, or people who have no permanent homes; they are wanderers. For thousands of years, the Sahel has been the home of different nomadic tribes. Now, most of them have disappeared. The Wodaabe, who live mainly in central Niger, remain among the last of the nomadic tribes of Africa—and of the world.

Because they live on the edge of the desert, where the land is too arid and the rainfall too uncertain to support agriculture, the Wodaabe are herders. They

In the Sahel, there is no rain
for nine months of the year.
The land is bare and cracked.

A deserted, drought-stricken village in Mauritania

depend upon their animals for their livelihood. Since water and pasture are scarce, these tribes travel across the countryside in search of food and water for their animals. Their wanderings usually follow a well-defined pattern. They travel from one known source of water and grazing land to another. A nomadic life is not easy. In the dry season, the Wodaabe often must walk 10 to 15 miles (15 to 25 km) a day, in temperatures as high as 120°F (49°C). Choosing to live as wanderers so that they can be "free to follow their own traditions," the Wodaabe have so far resisted all efforts by others to change their way of life. In small family groups of fifteen to thirty, they travel across the land, just as their ancestors have done for centuries.

Wodaabe homes are temporary, and their possessions are few. This is because everything they own must be carried on the backs of oxen. Their homes blend so well with the countryside that in the dry season it is possible to pass just a few yards away from a settlement without even realizing that it is there. In fact, among the settled people of the area, there is a saying describing the Wodaabe as "the wind that blows through the bush," because, when they leave a place, all that

The parched and sandy desert is
a difficult place in which to live.

A Wodaabe herdsman leading
a bull by the nose

Women of a Fulani village preparing
millet for the evening meal

remains is a few stripped branches and a patch of bare earth.

Besides the Wodaabe, other peoples live in central Niger. Among them are the Tuaregs, often called the "blue men of the desert" because they dye their clothes with indigo. The dye rubs off on their skins, making the Tuaregs look blue. The Tuaregs are traders as well as herders. Their camel caravans are a common sight as they travel across the desert from market to market.

The southern part of the Sahel is more fertile than the northern part. Farming is carried out in the south, as well as along the banks of rivers and around natural springs and wells. These naturally green areas are called *oases*. Many of these farmers belong to the Fulani tribe. The Wodaabe, too, are a part of the larger Fulani tribe. There are six million Fulanis in Africa. Earlier, many of them were nomads. Today, most of them live a *sedentary* or *semisedentary* existence; that is, they live in one place all year round, or move just once or twice in a year. Now, only the Wodaabe still remain nomads.

The Wodaabe are not regarded as being part of black Africa. Scholars are not sure of their origin. It is believed that they first appeared in the upper Nile basin and then traveled west. At the end of the 1800s, the Wodaabe fled Nigeria to avoid pressures from the British colonial rulers there, as well as pressures from local Muslim chiefs. The Wodaabe say that their ancestors chose the arid, hostile Sahel environment because here there would be no interference. They could then live and move as they pleased.

Although the Wodaabe speak the same language, Fulfulde, and follow the same religion, Islam, as the rest of the Fulani, they do not intermarry with their settled tribesmen. The Wodaabe are proud of their nomadic heritage, and they look down upon the settled Fulani. In folk stories told around the fire at night—a regular feature of Wodaabe life—settled Fulani and others are often made fun of. The Wodaabe prefer to keep to themselves, following their own customs and traditions.

Despite their different ways of living, the farmers and nomads have always been dependent upon each other. The Wodaabe nomads sell their milk, butter, and yogurt in villages, in exchange for cereals grown by the farmers, and other necessities.

HOW THE WODAABE LIVE

The Wodaabe travel in family groups of around thirty people. The group is large enough to give its members a sense of security, as well as a degree of protection against hostile tribes (cattle raids were common in earlier times). It is small enough, too, to move around easily and to be able to stay in one place for a period of time without using up the surrounding resources. And, being a small family group, it is usually a very closely knit one. Members help each other in times of trouble.

The Wodaabe family is made up of a man, his wives, and their children. Under the laws of Islam, a man is allowed up to four wives. This family forms a self-sufficient economic unit, being able to provide for practically all its needs.

*The Wodaabe travel in groups
with their few possessions.*

The wealth of the Wodaabe is measured by the number of cattle owned, not by money, and each man would like to own as many cattle as he can. In addition to cattle, a man of moderate wealth owns around ten oxen, and two to three mules to transport his possessions; a few dozen goats and sheep, which he sells or trades in the village; and a camel, which he rides across the desert. Of these, cattle are the main means of livelihood. For this reason, the Wodaabe rarely sell or eat their cattle. Thus, the Wodaabe eat beef only at feasts, and cattle are sold only to help a family get over hard times. The Wodaabe depend almost entirely on milk and milk products. Milk is their staple food, and Wodaabe women sell milk, butter, and yogurt in village markets. This is their main source of income.

Each Wodaabe family is a herd-owning, milk-selling enterprise, one in which every member plays an important role. There is a strict division of labor based on the sexes. The men look after the cattle, and the women manage the milk. Wodaabe men are in charge of the care, daily pasturing, and watering of cattle. It is the men who judge when the grazing grounds around a camp have run dry and decide when the group should move on in search of fresh pastures. The women milk the cows, convert milk into butter and yogurt, and are responsible for selling the products in the market. Although a woman can own cattle, they are officially part of her husband's or father's herd. She has no say in their upkeep, and it is the men who decide when to sell the women's cows. In the Wodaabe society, men are masters of the encampment while the women are mistresses of the home.

WODAABE HOMES

Although simple and temporary, the Wodaabe camp has a formal structure. A homestead always faces west. A curved back fence made of the branches of nearby trees defines the boundary. The fence also protects the home from roving animals and gives some privacy. Within the fenced area are the shelters (*suudi*) of the Wodaabe wives.

Each wife has her own shelter where she sleeps, raises her children, and keeps her belongings. A woman's shelter is her domain. It contains everything she owns: her bed, her hearth with its cooking utensils, leather sacks containing her clothes, perfumes, and jewelry, and a long wooden table on which rest her most valued possessions—her ceremonial *calabashes*. Calabashes are bowls, bottles, or dippers made from the hard-rinded fruit of the calabash vine. The fruit is dried and cut in half, and the insides are scraped out.

Wodaabe ceremonial calabashes are works of art. Women decorate them with beautiful, geometric designs that are supposed to protect the utensils as well as the owners. These designs are basically traditional, but each woman slightly varies the designs taught to her by her mother. Ceremonial calabashes are passed from one generation to the next, but they are never used. Whereas a Wodaabe man measures his wealth in cattle, a woman measures hers in calabashes. They are a woman's pride and joy and the object of her con-

A Wodaabe camp

A woman's pride is her calabashes, made from the fruit of the calabash vine.

stant attention. There is great rivalry among Wodaabe women for owning the best collection of calabashes.

Each woman cooks and cares for herself and her children. The husband takes turns eating with each of his wives. Young children sleep in their mother's shelter. As they grow older, boys sleep around the family campfire. Extra shelters are put up for the old women and visiting daughters. In front of the bed shelters is the calf rope, to which the cows of the household are tied. In front of these is the cattle corral, a clearing where the animals are grouped at night.

The entire Wodaabe homestead, consisting of the bed shelters, the calf rope,

and the cattle corral is called the *wuro*. The wuro is named after the head of the household, and the *suudu*, or shelter, after each wife. A woman's activities lie inside the calf rope, and a man's on the outside. Except for the head of the household, no man is allowed into the women's side of the calf rope.

WODAABE WORK

The rhythm of a man's day varies with the seasons. For most of the October to May dry season, the Wodaabe camp around wells. The pasture around the wells soon runs out, and the Wodaabe herders are forced to take their cattle far away in search of dwindling patches of pasture. The time between the seasons is hardest for the Wodaabe. The long dry season has come to an end, but the rains have not yet started. At this time, pasture is extremely hard to find. Water is available only in a few deep wells. Cows are undernourished and almost milkless. The Wodaabe often must sell their precious cattle at very low prices to buy millet to feed their families.

By June, life becomes less difficult. Occasional showers come to the Sahel, creating ponds and puddles, a source of water for the cattle. The Wodaabe are able to leave their wells and to camp beside these ponds. Although its movements seem haphazard to an observer, each family has a traditional territory and rarely moves outside of it.

Finally, in July, come the rains, reviving the parched land. For a short while, the countryside turns into a land of plenty. Everyone now moves toward the north. Bordering the Sahara, the north is the driest region of the Sahel. Here, pastures remain green for the shortest period. The Wodaabe use the pastures of the north first, before they dry up, and then gradually move toward the more fertile south, where the pastures remain green longer. In the wet season, both water and pastures are easily available, and the men often have time to sit and talk and to sip tea.

A woman's day, however, is more rigidly defined. Her day begins early, with the milking of the cows. After feeding her family its first meal of milk, she removes butter from the leftover milk and sours it. The soured milk will last longer, and she will sell some of it, along with the butter, in a nearby village. After she has cleaned

the calabashes from the morning's meal and brought water from a well or pond, she begins to pound the millet, a small-headed grain. In the dry season, when milk is scarce, Wodaabe women add millet to the family diet. They get the millet by trading their milk products with farming neighbors. The millet is ground into flour and then mixed with water and boiled. The women spend several hours each day grinding the millet with a wooden mortar and pestle, and their hands are always blistered from this work. Once boiled, the millet is eaten with milk or vegetables. Meat is eaten only occasionally.

Besides looking after the milking and feeding the family, Wodaabe women must take care of their homes. Keeping house in the desert is no easy task. Water must be carried, twigs must be found for firewood, and, because the Wodaabe are nomadic, possessions must be packed and unpacked constantly. When the Wodaabe set up camp, it is the women who must collect the bushes and build shelters. Since women do most of the work, a hardworking wife is highly valued, and the men are eager to acquire more wives.

Wodaabe couples are usually betrothed by their parents at birth. The betrothed couple must descend from the same line of ancestors, and marriage rituals stretch out over many years. They involve much gift giving and feasting. Since a wife is considered an asset, it is the boy's father who provides the gifts and feasts. The match is cemented only after a woman has her first child. Then the couple set up their own household. After that, a man is free to marry any other woman of his choice. These secondary marriages have little cere-

A Wodaabe group

mony surrounding them. In most cases, the killing of a ram is sufficient to formalize the match.

Children are very important to the Wodaabe, and a man with many children is highly respected. There is no school for the Wodaabe children. From a very young age, they learn by helping their parents. The boys become herders, and the girls help their mothers. Thus each child in a family means an extra helper for that family. In the uncertain nature of desert life, it is the family that supports and helps its members. Therefore, the larger the family, the more secure a man feels. The family cares for its sick and elderly, and it is the family that sees a man through hard times. Thus, if a man has no milk to feed his family, a relative, usually a brother or father, lends a cow. The borrower will return the cow only after it has given birth to calves, providing the borrower with a fresh source of income. In the long, harrowing droughts that are becoming a regular feature of the Sahel, however, this tendency for large families creates a greater food shortage for the Wodaabe.

WODAABE CUSTOMS AND BELIEFS

In contrast to their harsh surroundings, or perhaps as a result of these surroundings,

Although Wodaabe children don't attend school, other children of the Sahel do. Here a young boy carries his slate and other belongings.

the Wodaabe are a colorful people. They are extremely conscious of physical beauty. The Wodaabe appearance is striking. They are tall and graceful people, with high cheekbones and straight, sharp noses. The Wodaabe enhance their physical beauty by putting geometric tattoos on their faces. Men, women, and children all wear a profusion of beads and charms. The Wodaabe women wear eight brass hoops in each ear. These make a pleasant, jangling sound with each movement they take. Elaborate hair styles are also favored. Both men and women style their long hair into many small, tight braids. Besides looking attractive, the braids keep their hair free from grit and sand.

The everyday clothes of the Wodaabe are functional. Around their waists, the men wear a *dedo*. This is a tanned sheepskin decorated with silver studs. Over it, they wear a colored tunic. To protect their heads against the strong desert sun, the men wear wide-brimmed hats or bright turbans. They draw a piece of the turban across the mouth and nose to keep out sand stirred by the desert wind. The women wear wrappers of brightly dyed handwoven cloth that reach just below their knees. Except for younger women who want to appear flirtatious, most women do not cover their breasts. During festivals and celebrations, both men and women wear long, brightly colored robes. Stored carefully in leather bags for most of the year, these ceremonial robes, which the women spend many hours embroidering with elaborate designs, represent another form of Wodaabe art.

Because they must depend on each other for survival in times of crisis, the

Wodaabe place a high value on the strength of human relationships. They have strictly laid down rules of behavior for interpersonal as well as group relations. For the Wodaabe, life is rigidly governed by *pulaku*, the Fulani code. It tells the Wodaabe how to deal with his or her own tribe and family, as well as with others. The code explains how to treat parents, children, husbands, and wives. For example, a man and his wife can never show affection, call each other by name, or speak to each other personally during the day. People cannot look each other in the eye when they meet, and, although Wodaabe children are much loved, a parent must not play with or fondle his eldest children. The Wodaabe are ashamed of any lapse or break in their elaborate code of conduct.

Since they are at the mercy of a harsh environment, the Wodaabe believe that all events are governed by fate and must be borne with *hakkilo*, care and forethought; *munyal*, patience and fortitude; and *semteende*, reserve and modesty. These qualities are called for most during the October to May dry season.

For the Wodaabe, the rainy season is a time of celebration. The forced isolation of the dry season is over. Paths often cross, as everyone moves northward. Visiting friends and relatives becomes the favorite pastime. With plenty of water and pasture, life is freed, for a short while, from the daily grind for survival. Rams are slaughtered, and storytelling sessions—important to the Wodaabe because they have no written language—last far into the night.

WODAABE CELEBRATIONS

The Wodaabe hold their two yearly festivals at the height of the rainy season. First is the *worso*. People of the same lineage meet during the worso to celebrate births and marriages. An air of excitement fills the Wodaabe camps. Men show off their elaborate gowns, and women display their celemonial calabashes. The feasts and celebrations of the worso last for three days and nights. The *gerewol*, which follows a few weeks later, is even grander. For the gerewol, families of two lineages meet for a week of feasting and dancing.

The gerewol is a beauty contest among the men. The Wodaabe value male beauty more than female beauty. It is the men, the Wodaabe say, who have to woo the women. Young Wodaabe men spend hours painting their faces in preparation for each dance at the festival. They use yellow powder to lighten their skin and kohl—a kind of black eye liner—to emphasize the whites of their eyes. Lastly, they shave their hairlines and put a vertical line down their faces to create an elongated look. The Wodaabe consider this look beautiful.

Three unmarried young women, picked by the elders for their beauty, judge

With their faces made up, these young Wodaabe men are waiting to perform a dance during a festival.

the contest. Modestly, they cover their eyes with the left hand, pretending not to look at the dancing men. The men, in order to attract the attention of the women, resort to every body movement, facial expression, and chant that they can think of. After a period of observation, the young women select their favorites with a graceful wave of the hand. The winner receives no gifts, but he gains the admiration of the men and women at the gathering. The gerewol is the climax of the year for the Wodaabe. It is a time when old friends meet again, romances blossom—some of them leading to secondary marriages—and many cows are slaughtered. It is a time Wodaabe families will treasure and talk about often in the long, dry months ahead.

CHANGE COMES TO THE WODAABE

Traditionally, nomadic herding has been viewed as the most efficient method of land use in semiarid regions like the Sahel. With rare exceptions, the land cannot support farming. Therefore, a settled life style never developed. Herding cattle and living off milk products offered a greater possibility of survival in the dry Sahel environment than farming. This is what the Wodaabe have done for hundreds of years. Today, they choose to reject the temptation of modern ways, preferring to continue their unending trek across the Sahel.

The life style of the Wodaabe is now threatened, however. Societies throughout the world are facing change. Most are faced with the changes brought about by

technology. Many societies have radios, automobiles, and televisions, for example. The Wodaabe, however, are different. They have so far resisted the comforts that can be bought in a money economy. More important, they do not seem to want or need Western goods. Although small items like pins and eyelets are proudly used in the design of Wodaabe ceremonial dress, the Wodaabe buy mainly food and cloth from village markets.

Wodaabe camps show almost no signs of Western consumer goods. But change has begun, in the form of greatly increased numbers of cattle and humans. These greater numbers are placing strains on the availability of food and water. The Wodaabe life style is no longer the most efficient way of using the environment. It is, in fact, seen by environmental scientists as harming the environment. The reasons for this began many years ago, and the roots lie with Wodaabe culture and the effects of Western civilization.

Traditionally, the size of a man's herd of cattle was limited by natural causes. Water wells were few and far between, and cattle diseases were commonplace. Poor health conditions and constant war between the tribes also kept the human population down. Thus, there was a balance between the land and the people who lived off it.

The situation began to change in the late 1800s. During this time, many European countries wanted control over the riches of African lands and began to carve up Africa into colonies. The French took over the area of the Sahel and brought a number of improvements to the region. They improved health care for cattle as well as for humans and tried to make the land more fertile, too. They bored new wells in the countryside, and the cattle no longer died of thirst.

These improvements, though good in themselves, had important and, in the long run, unpleasant side effects. The human and cattle populations increased rapidly, while the amount of grazing land available remained the same. The delicate balance between the land and the life it was able to support was upset. The land has begun to wear out. Slowly, the Sahel is turning into a desert. This process is called *desertification*. It is due to the rise in animal and human population as well as extended years when there is little rain even in the wet season. It is taking place in many dry land areas the world over, where humans are overusing the vegetation and soil.

Desertification leads to soil erosion and a drop in the amount of vegetation in the area. The results are dramatic. Less than two hundred years ago, the Sahel was thickly forested. Today, it is an arid grassland, with great patches of bare earth. Experts have estimated that the Sahara desert is moving south at about 4 miles (6 km) a year. If no steps are taken, the entire Sahel will soon turn into a complete desert, as arid as the Sahara. Environmentalists are worried about this process of desertification and its results.

The Sahel runs through some of the poorest and least developed countries in the world. Because of this, the condition of the land remained largely unnoticed by the outside world. Then, a series of natural disasters suddenly brought this area into the limelight.

From 1967 to 1974 almost no rain fell in the Sahel. Although there was still water in a few wells, the pastures turned completely dry. Cattle began to die by the thousands. The Wodaabe, as well as other nomads in the region, lost their means of support. Aid from the United States, France, and other countries poured into the Sahel. Refugee camps were built and food was provided for thousands of starving people. Nomads of the region streamed into the camps. Once used to living in the wide open spaces, the nomads now lived crowded together in dirty, squalid conditions. Diseases swept through the refugee camps, killing hundreds of people. Children were hit especially hard. And, as one dry year followed another, the nomads began to lose hope of ever returning to their old way of life.

Finally, in 1974 the rains came. The Sahel turned green again. Most of the nomads left the camps with a few animals provided by the government and resumed their way of life. On the surface, things seemed to have returned to normal. There had been famines in the Sahel before, and the older people often talk about them. There was the "sale of children" famine (they sold those children they could no longer feed), "the grinding up of the water gourd" famine (they were forced to eat gourds), and the "sit and stroke your braids" famine (since there was nothing else to do). As their names indicate, they were all severe famines. But they passed, and for the Wodaabe, life continued as before. The famine of 1967 to 1974, however, was different. It had begun to change the nomad's way of life, a fact that the Wodaabe resented.

Some of the Wodaabe stayed on in refugee camps after 1974. They did not want to go back to the same uncertain way of life. They preferred to remain in the villages, although the famine had passed. Now, many of them work at jobs requiring few skills. Some sell good-luck charms and herbal cures—two areas in which the Wodaabe are said to be highly skilled. Others are unable to get jobs. They live in poverty on the edge of villages and are forced to beg for a living.

The people of the Sahel had barely had time to recover from the terrible years when another severe drought struck. From 1982 to 1984, there was almost no rain in the region. Once again, the nomads lost their herds and were forced to return to refugee camps. Once again, thousands of people were dying of hunger.

Governments of the stricken countries in the Sahel, as well as foreign aid agencies, want to put an end to these disasters. To do this, they are encouraging the nomads of the region to take up ranching. This means using new methods of raising cattle, fattening them, and selling them for meat. Ranching has been a successful method of land use in the western part of the United States and other arid regions. Ranching will limit the number of cattle in the Sahel and thus prevent overgrazing, one of the major causes of desertification. It will also result in settlement of the nomads into permanent locations.

The introduction of ranching in the Sahel has not met with success, however. For the Wodaabe, their cattle are more important than the money they would make by selling them for beef. For hundreds of years, they have seen their cattle as their main security and they are not convinced of the need to change. Besides, the Wodaabe love their cattle. A herder usually recognizes individual cattle by their voices, and even a young Wodaabe boy has an amazing degree of communication with his cattle. Thus, the Wodaabe continue to live life according to their age-old ways, and the slaughterhouses built by the government remain empty.

Change is inevitable. Once, this region had the world's largest nomadic population. The hardships of the last decades have forced many of these nomadic tribes to abandon their wandering ways. Over the years, the Wodaabe, too, are likely to adopt the use of money and a more settled way of life. That they have clung to the ways of their ancestors until today, in the face of great pressures, is in itself remarkable.

*Wodaabe men drawing
water from a well*

3

AUSTRALIA'S WESTERN DESERT

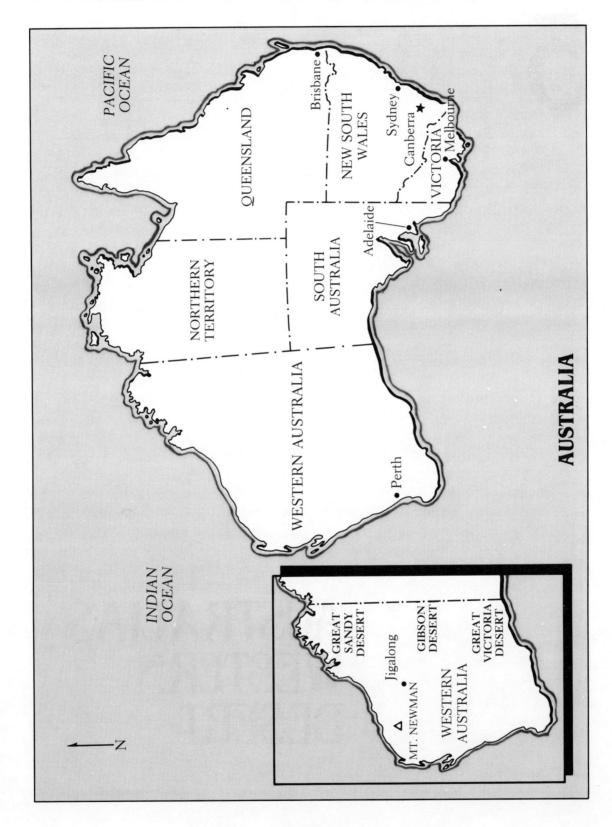

PACIFIC OCEAN

QUEENSLAND

NEW SOUTH WALES

Brisbane

Sydney

Canberra

Melbourne

VICTORIA

Adelaide

SOUTH AUSTRALIA

NORTHERN TERRITORY

WESTERN AUSTRALIA

Perth

INDIAN OCEAN

N

AUSTRALIA

GREAT SANDY DESERT

Jigalong

MT. NEWMAN

GIBSON DESERT

WESTERN AUSTRALIA

GREAT VICTORIA DESERT

One third of the entire continent of Australia is a desert. Of this, the Western Desert, which lies mostly in the state of Western Australia, is made up of the Gibson, the Great Victoria, and the Great Sandy deserts. All of these deserts run into each other. The Western Desert is an immense plateau that rises 1,000 feet (300 m) above sea level and stretches over 500,000 square miles (1,300,000 sq km). It is a land marked by low sandhills that run parallel to each other. These hills rise 100 to 300 feet (30 to 60 m) above the plateau, are cut by rugged, narrow gorges, and are separated from each other by areas of flat, sandy plains. Viewed from the top of the sandhills in the clear, sharp desert light, the land seems to stretch on forever, immense and unbroken.

Unlike the stereotype of the desert as a brown, bare land of shifting sand dunes, the Western Desert of Australia is a colorful place, dotted with vegetation. The bright red of the rocks and sandhills throws the various shades of green into sharp relief. Spinifex grass that grows on the ridges of hills, mulga shrubs, and stately desert oaks that rise to a height of 30 feet (10 m) can all be seen here. Multicolored birds—from small, noisy finches to large, flightless emus—weave in and out of mulga thickets and shrubs.

Despite its spectacular appearance, the Western Desert is a harsh and inhospitable land. Its climate is severe. For example, in the Gibson Desert, the summer temperatures can rise to 130° F (55° C)

in the shade. In the winter, night temperatures often fall below freezing. The air is rarely still; breezes and winds from different directions blow most of the day and sometimes also at night. Whirlwinds, which raise columns of dust and plant debris, are a common sight. The annual rainfall averages 5 to 10 inches (12 to 25 cm). But these statistics are misleading. Rainfall in the region is extremely uncertain. Sometimes there may be no rain at all for two to three years, and then several inches will fall in a single storm, flooding the entire area. Adding to the discomfort of the climate are the insects. Flies and ants abound, swarming over every living thing. Scorpions and snakes make the desert dangerous, too. To most people, the Western Desert is a barren, hostile environment. It is viewed as an enemy, one that must be tamed with the aid of technology, such as the air-conditioner and four-wheel-drive vehicle.

The first outsiders to enter the interior of the Western Desert were white adventurers. They came in the late 1800s in search of treasure, or in the hope of discovering fertile land. They all failed. Judging by their accounts, they considered themselves lucky to escape with their lives. When John Forrest crossed the Gibson Desert in 1874, he wrote: "We have not seen permanent water for the past eighty miles. . . . It is a most fearful country. . . . We can only crawl along having to lead the horses, or at least drag them." David Carnegie led a small party along the eastern edge of the Gibson Desert in 1896. Carnegie described the desert as a "vast, howling wilderness . . . words can give no (idea) of the ghastly desolation and hopeless dreariness of the scene which meets one's eyes from the crest of high ridge."

THE PEOPLE OF THE WESTERN DESERT: THE ABORIGINES

For over ten thousand years, the Western Desert has been the home of the Australian Aborigines. Until the late 1800s, the Aborigines had almost no contact with the rest of the world. The Aborigines of the Western Desert lived as nomads. They supported themselves entirely off the land. They were hunters and gatherers, and traveled across their territory in small family groups in search of food and water. The size of the group depended upon the availability of food and water. Sometimes, large groups from distant areas met at places where food and water were freely available. This was the high point of desert life, a time for important ritual ceremonies, for singing, dancing, and the exchange of ceremonial as well as other goods. Though nomads, the Aborigines retained—and still retain to this day—an attachment to specific areas that are thought of as their homelands.

Division of labor among the Aborigines was based on sex. Men hunted game and women and children collected plant foods such as grass seeds, berries, fruits, and roots. They also hunted for smaller game. While big game such as kangaroo was always shared by all the members of the group, vegetables and small game such as lizards and birds collected by the women were eaten by the immediate family. The old and the disabled who could not hunt or gather were fed by relatives. Cooking, which was done by the women, was a quick and easy task. Game was simply baked on hot ashes and sand. Most other food was eaten raw, and nothing was stored.

The desert was surprisingly rich in bird, insect, and animal life. This abundance, combined with the Aborigines' expert tracking abilities and their excellent knowledge of the environment, made food gathering a relatively easy task. In summer, in fact, work was done only in the early mornings, before the heat of the day began. The Aborigines rested in the afternoons to prevent loss of body water, a major hazard in the desert. Since their needs were so few, the task of survival was neither difficult nor time-consuming. There was plenty of time to play, to sing, and to dance. There was no urgency in aboriginal life, no battle against time in the quiet rhythm of their everyday lives.

The Aborigine material technology was among the least developed in the world. When white explorers first met them, the Aborigines had no domesticated animals, no metal tools, and no agriculture. They did not wear clothes. Their possessions were few. They used tools such as spears, *boomerangs*—curved clubs that can be thrown so that they return to the thrower—digging sticks, and dishes. These were lightweight, easy to carry, and made mostly of wood. The Aborigines did not build houses. Their shelter, when they

Tribesmen gather in small groups on the barren terrain of the outback. The clumps of vegetation serve as their only protection from the elements.

The Aborigines hunt animals with long spears made of bamboo and tipped with iron. Opposite: Flying foxes, fruit-eating members of the bat family, are relished by the Aborigines. Grandfather carves one up, while the young boy brings in another he has just caught.

camped, was a semicircle of branches—used to give shade in summer and act as a windbreak in winter.

An unusual aspect of the Aborigines' wandering pattern was the careful way in which they used their resources. The best water sources were least used. Waterholes were covered with branches to keep animals from falling in. When the Aborigines needed to make spears, they plucked the branches in such a way that the stem was not damaged. When rains made an area fertile, they moved to the very edge of that area and then gradually moved into it, "eating their way" into a camp and saving the best resources for the last.

The early white explorers believed that a people's technology was a sign of their intelligence. Because the Aborigines had a simple technology, the explorers thought these people were simpleminded. Their reports refer to the Aborigines as "wild, cruel black savages" and "the miserablest people in the world." One writer concluded that the Australian natives were almost wholly without religious feelings. He could not have been further from the truth. In contrast to their simple economic life, the Aborigines have a complex and rich religious and social structure. In fact, in order to understand the Aborigines' adaptation to their environment, it is necessary to try to understand their religion. Aborigine society was, and in some instances still is, a religious society. The Aborigines' religion explains their everyday life.

ABORIGINE BELIEFS

Over the centuries, the Aborigines developed a unique view of their environment.

White explorers saw the Western Desert as a barren wilderness. The Aborigines believed it was a beloved home, a friendly, secure place, shaped especially for them by a host of mythical beings. They agreed to live in the desert on its terms. They were certain that the desert would look after their needs as long as they lived their lives according to the "*Law*" set by their gods. In addition to this view of the environment, the Aborigines developed another belief. They believed in the harmony of the universe. For them, there was no difference between the natural world and the supernatural. They saw no difference between humans and their surroundings. Through their religion, they transformed their desert world into a friend and an ally. Thus, the Aborigines succeeded in surviving in a forbidding environment with ease and fluidity. And they did not feel the need for a highly developed technology.

In the past as well as in the present day, the most important part of Aborigine life is conformity to the Law. It was only conformity to the Law that ensured that rain would fall, plants would grow, and game would be abundant. The Aborigines wandered in small bands, not because the physical environment dictated this pattern of survival, but because that was the way their mythical ancestors—their gods—lived.

Central to Aborigine Law is the concept of the *Dreamtime*. According to Aborigine beliefs, the Dreamtime was the period of creation. It occurred long before the memory of the oldest living people. During the Dreamtime the ancestral beings transformed Australia from a flat, featureless plain and gave it its distinctive landmarks. For the Aborigines, the desert is crisscrossed with the tracks of these ancestral creative beings. According to the Aborigines, these beings are part animal and part human. They also have supernatural powers. They fought, hunted, danced, and behaved much as their descendants, the desert Aborigines did, but in doing so, they threw up the high hills and created the winding creek beds and waterholes that mark the land.

Every aboriginal group attributes the landmarks in its area to the adventures of its heroes. These adventures are incorporated into the songs, dances, and rituals of the group, as the following example shows:

They travelled along . . .
    To the Place of Honey they came.
They rested and arose.
    They travelled on.
To the Mad Place they came and passed it.
    They pressed on
And reached Thigh Place and drank.
    Again they travelled on
And came to Message Stick and turned,
    They travelled north
And came to Two Daughters
    There they camped.

Most of the paintings of the Aborigines are abstract. Sometimes they have secret meanings, sometimes they tell stories of ancestors. This painting shows the "life of the tribe."

*Young Aborigines prepare
for a traditional dance.*

Since the Aborigines have no written language, the songs serve also to familiarize the people with their surroundings, so that through the songs a young person who has never visited his or her homeland will know its landmarks, and the order in which they occur.

Ritual activity ensured the well-being of the aboriginal group. Because of this, it was of great importance. Rituals that ensured plentiful food and water were carried out by the men and kept secret from the women and children. Since women did most of the work, the men spent their time preparing for and carrying out these rituals. Their ceremonial boards and other

ritual objects were elaborately carved or painted with natural dyes. Men enjoyed a higher status than women because they were seen as the ones who nourished and maintained the land through their practice of the rituals. It was only by conducting these rituals and by following the Law laid out during the Dreamtime that Aborigines felt they could control their environment.

THE ABORIGINES TODAY

As is the case with most small-scale, distinctively different societies the world over—the American Indians being a close

A group of Aborigines in ceremonial paint perform one of their ancient ritual dances, known as corroborees.

parallel—the Aborigines have not been able to withstand the influence of the outside world. Today, the Aborigines of the Western Desert are no longer nomads. Most of them live in settlements on the edge of the desert.

Jigalong, in the north-central state of Western Australia, is one such settlement. In his book, *The Jigalong Mob: Aboriginal Victors of the Desert Crusade*, Professor Robert Tonkinson—one of the few people to have studied the Jigalong settlement—writes that the history of the aboriginal settlement in Jigalong is more or less similar to that of other settlements throughout the Western Desert area. In the early 1900s, small outposts of white settlements began to be built along the edge of the Western Desert. They were mainly cattle and sheep ranches, mining settlements, railroad centers, and missions. In 1907 a fence was built across vast areas of the Western Desert in order to prevent rabbits from invading certain areas of the continent. Jigalong was a small *depot*, or supply station, set up to maintain the fence. It was located in an area of favorable water and game supplies.

By 1930, desert Aborigines had begun to drift into Jigalong. At first they came out of curiosity. They wanted to see what the white settlers were doing. Gradually, older Aborigines, probably tempted by the ease of obtaining food, stayed on in Jigalong. Because of this, the depot superintendent was made a "Protector of Natives." He was authorized by the government to issue food rations to nearby Aborigines. Also, the depot made it a policy to give jobs to as many Aborigines as possible, in return for ration handouts.

Aborigines continued to come to Jigalong. Some came out of curiosity, others because they needed food.

Most of the Aborigines viewed their stay in Jigalong as temporary. They intended to return to their homelands. Soon, however, they became accustomed to the settled life style. They also developed a taste for civilized foods, such as flour, sugar, and tea, and for tobacco. This emigration continued into the 1960s. Now, there are no Aborigines living in the interior of the Western Desert.

LIFE IN JIGALONG

Jigalong, which stands at the meeting of two creek beds, is located within a 500,000 acre (200,000 ha) *Native Reserve*. In a Native Reserve, Aborigines can come and go as they please, but outsiders are allowed in only with special permission from the government. There are two distinct settlements at Jigalong, separated by Jigalong Creek. On one side of the creek lie the buildings constructed by the white settlers. These include a store, a hospital, a school, and other such support systems. On the other side of the creek is the Aborigine camp. In contrast to the well-built, neatly-laid-out buildings, the Aborigine camp is a haphazard collection of structures made of canvas, bushes, and poles. These are temporary shelters and are moved whenever the surrounding area becomes dirty. Litter, abandoned vehicles, and groups of scavenging dogs add to the general feeling of disarray. Water is pumped in by means of windmills from wells about a mile (1.6 km) away from the camp. But the water in these wells is not

Government housing for Aborigines

abundant, and there is often a water shortage in the area.

Aborigine houses in Jigalong are spaced according to language groups. Although the Aborigine culture was similar throughout the Western Desert, a few language differences did develop over the years. Thus, the Aborigines at Jigalong speak different *dialects*; that is, they speak slightly different varieties of the same language. However, they all identify themselves as Jigalong Aborigines.

Jigalong is relatively isolated. The settlement is linked to the outside world only by poor-quality gravel roads. Supplies have to be brought in by truck from a railroad center 300 miles (485 km) south, and the mail is infrequent. Except for government officials, the *Flying Doctor service*, and Aborigines from nearby desert settlements, Jigalong people receive few visitors from the outside world.

Weather conditions in Jigalong are desertlike. The summers are long and hot, and rainfall is scanty. Game is abundant in the area, and kangaroos, emu, and lizards are still commonly hunted. Vegetation around Jigalong, however, has been completely worn away by the constant use of the land. Because the Aborigines no longer depend directly upon the land, the barren countryside with its exposed topsoil is not a threat to them. In earlier times, the roots, shrubs, and insects of the region were a major part of the Aborigine diet. Their disappearance, therefore, would have had serious results for the nomadic people. Today, the Aborigines work for money and buy their food from stores. Thus, the wearing away of the land has become just a minor inconvenience.

Most of the Aborigines of Jigalong today eat three meals a day; originally they ate only one. Although they now rely heavily on nonaboriginal foods, their cooking methods are a blend of the old and the new. Placing game directly on hot ashes is still the most popular method of cooking. Pots and pans are sometimes used to make stews or other complicated dishes.

There are not too many job opportunities for the Aborigines of Jigalong. Most of them work in nearby cattle stations (the Australian term for ranches). However, the cattle stations cannot afford to employ the Aborigines throughout the year, and they still live at Jigalong between jobs. The men work as drivers, cattle herders, and stock handlers, or do odd jobs around the stations. The women usually work as housemaids and cooks. Older people, most of whom receive government pensions, and mothers with young children live permanently in Jigalong.

Everyone in the settlement wears western clothes: trousers, dresses, sweaters, and shoes. Most of these are bought secondhand from the local store. Younger people spend a lot of money on their appearance. For young Aborigine men, the "cowboy" image of hats, boots, jeans, and guitars is a popular one.

The Aborigines do not earn much money. What they do earn, they spend primarily on food and clothes. Very little is spent on durable items, except those that are considered necessities. Cooking utensils, knives, and flashlights are most in demand. Saving for the future is not part of the aboriginal culture. Whatever money the Aborigines have left over, they spend on gambling, drinking, and gift-buying. Rifles, radios, and secondhand vehicles are the most expensive items bought by the Aborigines.

To outward appearances, the Aborigines of Jigalong have adopted a western life style. But these appearances are deceptive. For though their settled life style and their economic dependence on whites has led to changes in their culture, the Aborigines of Jigalong have kept their basic values. They perform all important rituals and activities. They keep close spiritual ties with their home territory. They depend upon the age-old kinship codes for their relationships with each other. In fact, the middle-aged and older Aborigines of Jigalong are mainly concerned with the preservation of their traditions; that is, the Law. They have a strong sense of their identity and are proud of the fact that neighboring aboriginal communities look upon them as keepers of the Law.

The ability of the Aborigines at Jigalong to keep their traditions is in sharp contrast to the collapse of aboriginal culture in most other areas of Australia. Many aboriginal societies have fallen apart completely, and demoralized Aborigines have taken to heavy drinking and gambling. Although drinking and gambling do pose a problem in Jigalong, it is far less of a problem than in other aboriginal communities.

Today, Jigalong is one of the last places in Australia where old traditions are still central to the Aborigines' world view. The reasons for this have a lot to do with the environment around Jigalong.

When British colonists came to Australia in the 1700s, they first occupied the fertile areas of the continent. Believing the Aborigines to be little better than animals, the colonists paid little attention to their fate. The Aborigines were forced off their land and often physically attacked. Shocked by the sudden and brutal culture contact, the Aborigines fell apart completely. The few who survived were forced to live on the fringes of white society.

The desert remained untouched, however. The harsh physical conditions prevented the colonists from settling there, and, except for a few explorers in the late 1800s, whites rarely ventured into the Australian interior. White explorers who did venture into the Western Desert were often forced to rely upon the excellent tracking abilities of the Aborigines to lead them to water. Thus, the Aborigines of the Western Desert did not feel inferior to the whites. Also, unlike their counterparts in eastern and southern Australia, the Aborigines of the Western Desert were not forced off their land. Their contact with the whites was, in most cases, voluntary. It was the Aborigines who moved into the settled areas on the edge of the desert, then decided to stay in white settlements. In the desert, the Aborigines had time to get used to the ways of the white settlers.

From 1947 to 1969, Jigalong was a mission station. For twenty-four years the missionaries tried to convert the Aborigines to Christianity. Their efforts failed completely. In 1970 the settlement was taken over by the Australian government, and in 1973 it became an incorporated aboriginal community. The Aborigines elected an all-Aborigine council to run their settlement. Although they depend on the help of the white advisers, the Aborigines have begun to have a say in their own affairs for the first time since they left the interior.

THE FUTURE OF
THE ABORIGINES

After many years of ignoring and often mistreating them, white Australians have begun to become aware of the Aborigines' problems. In 1984 the Australian government set aside over 300 million dollars (equal to about 200 million U.S. dollars) for special programs for the Aborigines. The government is also encouraging the Aborigines to deal with their own community problems. More important, the people of Australia are beginning to realize the uniqueness of Aborigine traditions and the importance of preserving them. Jigalong is witnessing the benefits of these new policies. For example, housing and health care improvements are under way. A more enlightened educational policy is being adopted. Aboriginal languages are taught to the children in schools, and aboriginal elders are asked to speak to the children about traditional ways. Aboriginal teachers' aids are employed, and white teachers are instructed to try to understand the background of the aboriginal children. Adult education has also been started.

The discovery of mineral deposits in the area may bring more changes to Jigalong. In 1970, iron-ore mining operations were started at Mount Newman, 100 miles (160 km) west of Jigalong. Although few Jigalong people are actually employed in the mines, it is possible that minerals will be discovered closer to Jigalong. This will put a quick end to the unique isolation of Jigalong.

In 1977, Aborigines at Jigalong made a lands claim on their traditional home territories, which lie in the interior of the Western Desert. Aboriginal homelands that lie in remote, sparsely populated areas of Australia are now being returned to the respective Aboriginal communities by the Australian government. This land is then owned by those Aboriginal communities. Land claims in some states of Australia, such as the Northern Territory, have already been granted. Those of Western Australia are still under consideration. The granting of land claims may lead to *decentralization*. This means that the Aborigines may take up living in small groups near waterholes, as a few aboriginal groups from other areas of Australia have begun to do.

Improved communication and an increasing awareness of the outside world are changing the Aborigines' way of life. No one can be sure in what way the Aborigines will change. Unlike their counterparts in the rest of Australia, the Aborigines at Jigalong have used their isolation to their advantage. They have had time to get used to the ways of the larger white society. They have, so far, been able to keep their sense of identity and a hopeful outlook. Because their environment has changed, they have changed with it—they wear clothes, their children go to school, they shoot game with rifles—but they still see themselves as traditional Aborigines, as keepers of their Law. They have changed only the part of their lives that they feel does not conflict with their Law.

A bark petition presented to the Australian government by two Aborigine elders seeking land rights for their people

*Above: Aboriginal elders meet to discuss matters affecting their people.
Opposite: The Aborigines have been active in trying to claim homelands lying in remote areas of Australia.*

JAN14th-15th
ABORIGINAL LAND RIGHTS

VIGIL
VIGIL

24-HOUR SILENT VIGIL OUTSIDE COMMONWEALTH PARLIAMENTARY OFFICES MARTIN PLACE

THURSDAY 14TH JANUARY 5 P.M. TO FRIDAY 15TH JANUARY 5 P.M.

TO DEMAND LAND RIGHTS FOR ABORIGINES. Contact: Land Rights. Box 66, Potts Point. 2011

Authorised by A. Tate, 26 Bon Accord Avenue, Bondi Junction.

JOIN US IF YOU BELIEVE IN HUMAN RIGHTS

As a result, they are proving an inspiration to Aborigines in other areas.

Whether the Aborigines at Jigalong are able to create a place for themselves as a cultural minority will depend upon two things: their ability to keep adjusting to changing social and economic conditions, and the white Australian society's willingness to accept and promote Aboriginal growth.

4

NORTE
GRANDE

THE
CHILEAN
DESERT

64

CHILE AND ARGENTINA

PERU

BOLIVIA

BRAZIL

TARAPACÁ

Tocopilla

Chuquicamata

Chiu Chiu

San Pedro
de Atacama

PARAGUAY

ANTOFAGASTA

ATACAMA

ARGENTINA

URUGUAY

Santiago

PACIFIC
OCEAN

ANDES MOUNTAINS

CHILE

VENEZUELA

GUYANA

SURINAM

FR. GUIANA

COLOMBIA

ECUADOR

PERU

BRAZIL

BOLIVIA

PARAGUAY

CHILE

URUGUAY

ARGENTINA

N

Atacama Desert

Chile is a long, narrow country stretching for 2,900 miles (4,640 km) along the Pacific coast of South America. From the air, it looks like a giant, scalloped ribbon. Because of its great length, the climate and vegetation differ dramatically from north to south. To the north is the Chilean desert, called Norte Grande, or the "Great North." It extends over 600 miles (960 km) and is part of the coastal desert of South America that reaches upward into Peru and Ecuador. In the center of Chile lie fertile farmlands, and in the south there are dense forests. From west to east also, Chile can be divided into three sections. From the northern desert down to the deep south, Chile is broken up into a coastal belt of mountains, the *cordillera* of the Andes, and a central valley that lies between these two mountain ranges. Since the average breadth of Chile is only about 105 miles (170 km), most places in the country have a backdrop of mountains and hills on either side.

Norte Grande is one of the driest places on earth. There are weather stations in this desert where rainfall has never been recorded. Except for a few river valleys and oases, it is a bleak, barren land with no vegetation except for lichen and cactus. The naturalist Charles Darwin called Chile's Norte Grande the "most complete and utter desert." In this region, the coastal mountains are steep and craggy. They rise to a height of 7,000 feet (2,100 m) and then drop sharply into the ocean, leaving little room for natural harbors.

The Great North is made up of the provinces of Tarapaca, Antofagasta, and Atacama. In the plains, the days are hot and the nights extremely cold throughout the year. However, closeness to the ocean and the cooling Humboldt Current that runs through it has a moderating effect on the climate of the area. Temperatures rarely rise above 85° F (30° C), and there is little difference between summer and winter temperatures.

Although the Great North makes up almost one-third of the area of Chile, it contains only about 8 percent of its population. Because of the lack of water, few people have settled in the area. Most of them live in a few cities and towns. The rest of the desert remains empty and brown, a vast expanse of sand and rock.

The central belt of Chile is its heartland. It is a region made up of bustling cities, busy ports, and fertile farmlands. Despite this, it is the Great North that is vital to the country's economy. This is because Chile's desert region is rich in minerals. Today, Chile's most important mineral is copper. The world's largest copper deposit has been discovered in this area. In addition, dried up lake beds contain *caliche*, a raw form of *sodium nitrate*, a mineral salt that is used as a fertilizer. Also, the volcanoes of the Andes are topped with high-grade sulfur ores. For almost 200 years, Chile's economy has depended upon the export of minerals, mainly from the Great North. Because of this, the region has played an important

*Above: Coastal fog in the
waterless desert in Chile.
Opposite: Harvesting salt*

role in the history of the nation. Wars have been fought, elections lost and won, and thousands of mine workers have died over the fate of this barren, windswept desert.

THE PEOPLE OF CHILE

Lured by reports of great mineral wealth, the Spanish invaded Chile in the 1500s. They entered the country from Peru and had great difficulty crossing the Chilean desert. Finally, they came upon the fertile, temperate lands of Chile's central valley. Although they did not discover the gold and silver that they had come for, the Spanish decided to stay there.

At that time, Chile was peopled with different groups of Indians. Each of these groups had its own language and culture. Because the early Spanish settlers had few women with them, they intermarried with the local Indians. Their descendants, called *mestizos*, now form a majority of the country's population. Chilean society has a strong class system. It is very difficult for people to move into a higher class. There is a small upper class, a sizable middle class, and a large lower class. The upper class is made up of land-owning Spanish families as well as small groups of later European immigrants who have chosen not to intermarry with Indians or mestizos. These people have always controlled Chile's wealth.

Traditionally, Chilean society was based upon huge land holdings owned by the elite. Concentrated in the central valley and often running into tens of thousands of acres, these estates, called *haciendas*, were served by tenant farmers. Each hacienda was a self-contained unit, with its own store, church, and school. There was little opportunity for the workers outside the hacienda, and those who left it were called *rotos*, or "broken ones," because of the tragic fate that awaited them outside the security of the estate. Most of these rotos left the estates to work in the mines of the north.

Today haciendas are no longer the center of Chilean life. Workers streamed into the cities in search of a better life, and now over 80 percent of Chile's population live there. While the rich live in huge houses equipped with modern conveniences, the poor live in slum tenements and makeshift huts. Most of Chile's 11.5 million people are concentrated in the fertile central valley. In fact, 44 percent of all Chileans live in or around the capital city of Santiago. This is because both the north and the south of Chile have extreme climates. The north is too dry and barren to offer an easy life to its residents; the south is too wet and densely forested.

Spanish is the national language of Chile. Literacy is higher in Chile than in most South American countries. Over 80 percent of the people know how to read and write. Most Chileans are devout Roman Catholics, and religion plays an important role in the life of the people, as well as in the politics of the country.

THE IMPORTANCE OF MINERALS

The Spanish conquerers came to Chile in search of precious minerals. They passed the desert by, however, thinking it a waterless wasteland. The face of Chile's desert remained unchanged until the 1800s, when nitrate, which is abundant in the area, was found to be a good fertilizer. The country flourished from the money earned from nitrate's export. Mining towns, ports, and railroads came into being as a result of the nitrate industry, and the Chilean desert began to be developed. Then, in 1920, synthetic nitrate was developed. The synthetic variety was found to be cheaper than the natural substance. By 1929, the Chilean nitrate industry was almost out of business. Less than 5 percent of the original plants are operating today. Ghost towns, abandoned railroad lines, and dumps scattered across the desert are all that remain of the great nitrate boom.

Now, copper is the leading product of Chile's north. It has been a key factor in the development of the desert and in the Chilean economy. In 1983, copper represented 48 percent of the overall exports of the country, with foreign sales of over 1.8 million dollars. Most of Chile's copper comes from three large mines. Chuquicamata, the largest of these mines, supplies 60 percent of all Chile's copper.

CHUQUICAMATA— THE WORLD'S LARGEST OPEN PIT MINE

Located in the province of Antofagasta, Chuquicamata is the world's largest open pit mine. The pit is 2 miles (3 km) long, half a mile (0.8 km) wide, and over a thousand feet (300 m) deep. More than 100,000 tons of copper-bearing ore and waste rock are removed daily from this pit. The low-grade copper ores of Chuquica-

mata have proven to be the greatest known reserves of the metal. Experts say there is enough ore at the mine to continue operations for more than one hundred years. Chuquicamata sits in the middle of the Chilean desert. Since there is no water in Chuquicamata, it is impossible for humans to survive there without outside help. Yet this wasteland has been turned into a thriving, bustling city.

CHUQUICAMATA— AS A PLACE TO LIVE

In Chuquicamata, they say the desert has been conquered. This city of over thirty thousand people has all the trappings of a modern metropolis—auditoriums, churches, schools, theaters, clubs, shops, and hospitals. It has electricity as well as adequate telephone service with the outside world. Houses of red brick and stone with corrugated iron roofs are laid out in neat rows, and the city's paved streets are lined with pepper trees.

The amazing thing about Chuquicamata is that everything, from the soil used to plant trees to the water and food consumed by the people, must be brought in across the desert. The transport of supplies is difficult as well as very expensive. For example, beef is brought by way of cattle trucks all the way from Argentina. The cattle make the twenty-four hour journey across the trans-Andean highway that connects the Antofagasta Province with Salta in Argentina. Because beef is an important part of the Chilean diet, the trip is seen as being worth the expense. Vegetables and fruits for Chuquicamata are now being grown in nearby oases like

Above: A conveyor belt at Chuquicamata
transports copper ore from the mine to
the crushing plant. Opposite: Copper being
loaded on a ship in Antofagasta destined
for the United States

San Pedro de Atacama and Chiu Chiu. The growth of Chuquicamata has affected these places too. Now, instead of engaging in the subsistence farming they have practiced for centuries, the farmers are growing food and vegetables to sell to Chuquicamata. In the process, these farmers are emerging from years of isolation.

THE IMPORTANCE OF WATER

The development of water resources has been essential to the growth of mining settlements such as Chuquicamata. Three rivers from the snow-clad Andes drain towards the Pacific. Only one of these, the Rio Loa, reaches the Pacific Ocean. The other two are absorbed by the desert. In addition to these, there are numerous springs in the desert. Considering the almost complete lack of rainfall and high rate of evaporation in this region, scientists were intrigued by this relative abundance of springs in the northern desert. Investigating this, engineers at Chuquicamata discovered that water that fell as rain or snow as much as a hundred years ago on the eastern range of the Andes Mountains drained underground, to emerge as springs at the foot of the volcanoes in the Chilean desert.

Five pipelines carry water from these springs and rivers to Chuquicamata. The mining industry requires a great deal of water. This, coupled with rising standards of living, creates an ever-growing demand for water. This demand has begun to strain the available resources. Because water supplies must go first to mining areas, surrounding agricultural settlements

have had to make do with smaller supplies. This in turn means that fewer crops are grown in the region and results in the additional expense of bringing foods in from far away.

Chile's oil and coal reserves, as well as most of its sources for *hydroelectric power*, or water power, are located mainly in the far south. The great length of the country makes it uneconomical to connect pipelines from the south to isolated centers in the north. As a result, mining companies usually have their own electrical generators. Chuquicamata gets its energy from a steam turbine plant at nearby Tocopilla. The mine also gets energy from *waste smelter heat*, that is, the heat that escapes from molten metal. However, as a result of a rapidly growing population and a demand for electrical appliances, power generation is having a difficult time keeping up with increasing demand. Scientists are investigating the possibilities of expanding hydroelectric power and developing *geothermal*, heat from the earth, and solar energy sources.

THE HISTORY OF CHUQUICAMATA

In the words of Chile's former president Salvador Allende Gossins, copper provides the "salary of Chile." Because of this, the management of copper mines has played an important role in the politics of the country.

In the early 1900s United States copper companies bought and developed Chuquicamata and other large copper mines. Although the Chilean government received funds in the form of taxes, it had

Only a few miles from Chuquicamata,
Indians live in much the same way as their
ancestors did. This woman is weaving.

In the Chilean desert pipelines must carry water to Chuquicamata from springs and rivers far away.

little to say in the development and management of the mines. The people of Chile began to resent the foreign ownership of their precious metal. In 1964, the government of Chile began a series of talks with the American owners of the large mines. As a result, in the late 1960s, the government acquired part ownership of the large mines. By 1970, Chile was getting 83 percent of the earnings of Chuquicamata and other large mines, as well as a degree of control in their planning and operation. This program was called Chileanization.

In 1970, President Salvador Allende Gossins, the country's first Marxist leader, won the elections partly on his promise to *nationalize*, to bring under the control of the national government, the copper mines. In 1971 all copper mines were taken over by the government of Chile and placed under the direct supervision of the State Copper Corporation (CODELCO). Thus CODELCO became the largest copper company outside of the Soviet Union. In 1973 a new government came into power under the leadership of General Augusto Pinochet Ugarte. Pinochet, who believes in free market economics, sold most of the copper mines to private owners. The three largest mines, including Chuquicamata, however, were kept under government control.

THE PEOPLE OF CHUQUICAMATA

The people of Chuquicamata are not traditionally a desert people. The people of the Chilean desert are Indians who have lived around oases and farmed small plots

of land for centuries. They continue to do this. Just as food and water must be brought in over great distances to Chuquicamata, its people too, have come from the south.

In the early 1900s, when nitrate began to be mined in the north, many tenant farmers left their haciendas and came to the desert region in the hope of bettering their lives. They were bitterly disappointed, however. Conditions in the mining towns were often worse than on the haciendas that they had fled. They were made to toil long hours in the harsh desert climate, and they were paid hardly enough to survive. Since everything had to be transported long distances, even food was very expensive. Thus, the cost of living was much higher than in the south.

There were other difficulties, too. The hacienda functioned as a tightly knit community. In the mining towns, the workers found themselves suddenly cut off from this supportive group. There were no other recreational facilities available to occupy their minds, either. Almost in desperation, the miners of the north organized themselves into a union and demanded higher wages and better living and working conditions. Until then, Chile's lower classes had never had a say in their own affairs. Thus, their demands were ignored by the mine owners and government authorities. The miners began to strike in protest. These strikes were often put down with force. For example, in the first major strike of nitrate workers in 1907, over two thousand workers were killed by government forces.

The conditions in the desert served to strengthen the unity of the workers.

The concentration of large groups of wage workers in isolated settings helped forge a militant, powerful, and highly political labor force. The protests and strikes of the miners continued, in spite of repression by mine owners, backed by government forces. The struggle to achieve a better life spread from the mining camps to the ports and railroads that supported the mining industry. From the desert region, the workers' struggle spread to the south. Union organizers of the north became the national leaders of the Chilean working class. They carried their demand for higher wages and better living conditions from the desert to the centers of economic and political power in the south.

Union activity continued until the 1970s, in spite of government and employers' efforts to limit union power. Today, 60 percent of all miners and 40 percent of all industrial workers in Chile are unionized. The copper miners' union now has twenty-two thousand members, and is one of the best organized and most powerful of all workers' unions in Chile. Unions have become a major political force in the country. After the Pinochet government came into power in 1973, it tried to suppress all union activity and suspended trade union rights.

The unions did not give up, however. They continued to protest, and finally the government was forced to compromise. A new labor plan was put into effect in 1979. Workers were allowed to strike and to elect their own leaders. Their powers have been greatly cut back, though. For example, if they strike for more than sixty days, they are likely to lose their jobs. Not willing to accept these terms, the copper miners protested, and in the resulting strike, twelve hundred copper miners lost their jobs.

In June 1984, the army moved into Chuquicamata to prevent its workers from going on another strike. It appears that the struggle of the people of Chuquicamata is far from finished. However, in the past one hundred years, the workers of the northern desert have succeeded in changing the social fabric of the country, one that had existed for centuries. The workers of Chile have now become a powerful group, a force to be reckoned with.

CONDITIONS IN CHUQUICAMATA TODAY

The miners are the cream of Chile's labor force, and the workers of Chuquicamata are among the best paid in the country. They are provided with houses and medical and recreational facilities. It is their compensation for living in the inhospitable desert.

In the past few years, Chile's economy has suffered, partly because of a falling world price for copper. People in Chuquicamata are finding it difficult to make ends meet. Because of the present government's policies, the miners are insecure about their jobs and morale is low. Many community clubs have developed in the past few years, and these give moral as well as monetary support to the miners. The Church has also helped the workers in their struggle, and, because of this, many priests have been in trouble with the Pinochet government.

The city of Antofagasta

An Indian and his wife in their house

The family is another source of help and comfort. Family ties have always been strong in Chile, and now, in times of trouble, families are banding together. Cousins, aunts, uncles, and married children are moving in together, so that more wage-earning members can bear the burden of supporting the family. Women, too, have begun to take jobs. Chilean society is a traditional one, and women usually work as domestic servants or seamstresses, or at other such jobs considered suitable for women. They do not work in the mines.

The people worst hit by the hard times, however, are the squatters. During the early 1950s, a construction project brought a large number of workers and their families from other parts of Chile to Chuquicamata. These people refused to return to their former homes when the work was finished. They felt they had better prospects in Chuquicamata. They built themselves homes out of discarded materials and stayed on. Later, people from the surrounding villages began to drift in. Because most of the available water was being used by Chuquicamata, the farms of the surrounding villages began to dwindle. The Indians from these villages were forced to come to Chuquicamata to search for jobs. These people, too, stayed in the shantytowns surrounding the city.

These squatters try to find work as domestics, chauffeurs, repairmen, or doing odd jobs, but this is not always possible. Because of the high rate of unemployment, the frustrated people of these shantytowns often take to drinking and crime. Although the government is trying to provide housing and medical aid for these people, it is not enough to meet the growing demand.

In the future, Chuquicamata will continue to grow. If it is not to do so at the expense of the surrounding communities, it must use its water sparingly. The growing shantytowns as well as the low morale of the miners are other problems that will have to be solved in the coming years.

5

A
COMPARISON
OF
THREE
DESERT
REGIONS

The desert dictates its terms: humans cannot face its rigors alone. In order to survive, they must seek the help of others. You see this in the three desert communities you have examined. Both Wodaabe and aboriginal culture stress cooperation with the band. In Chuquicamata too, it is only by organizing themselves that the miners are able to live and work in the desert.

Traditionally, scarcity of water, and therefore, of food, have been key factors in shaping the way of life in the desert. The technological breakthroughs of the twentieth century have lessened people's dependence on their surroundings. Air-conditioning and airplane and auto travel have made desert living and travel less fearsome. But the new life style has created its own problems. It has led to the overuse and pollution of existing resources. This calls for new ways of survival.

To understand the present life of the desert communities, it is necessary to examine the changes of the past hundred years in the setting of traditional ways. All the communities you have studied have evolved different ways of living within their desert environment. There are two main reasons for this. The environment—the climate and the amount of food and water available—differs in each of these areas. Also, each community views its environment in a different way and adjusts to it accordingly.

Both the Wodaabe and the Aborigines of Jigalong were nomads, but with a difference. The Aborigines were hunter-gatherers. That is, they roamed the countryside in order to feed themselves. They had no animals, very few possessions, and no personal wealth. They moved within a specific area, and they were deeply attached to this area. In folk tales and poems, each group's special territory was referred to as its homeland. There were very few Aborigines in the Western Desert, and they had a deep knowledge of their environment. Because of this, they were able to find enough food and water for their needs. Thus, for thousands of years, Aborigines of the Western Desert lived a simple life, free of the trappings of civilization.

The Wodaabe are herders. In a sense, they are one step removed from the land: they depend upon the land to feed their animals. The animals in turn feed them. Because they own animals, the Wodaabe have a more complex life style. A family counts its wealth by the number of animals it owns.

The Wodaabe need clothes, too, to protect them against the hot desert sun. In hot, arid areas, loss of body water through evaporation is great, and clothes become a necessary protection. The Aborigines did not have to work during the heat of the day, and so they had no need to cover their bodies. The Wodaabe, however, must take their cattle long distances in search of food and water. This calls for many hours in the blazing sun. Thus, clothes are needed. The Wodaabe get these in the village markets in exchange

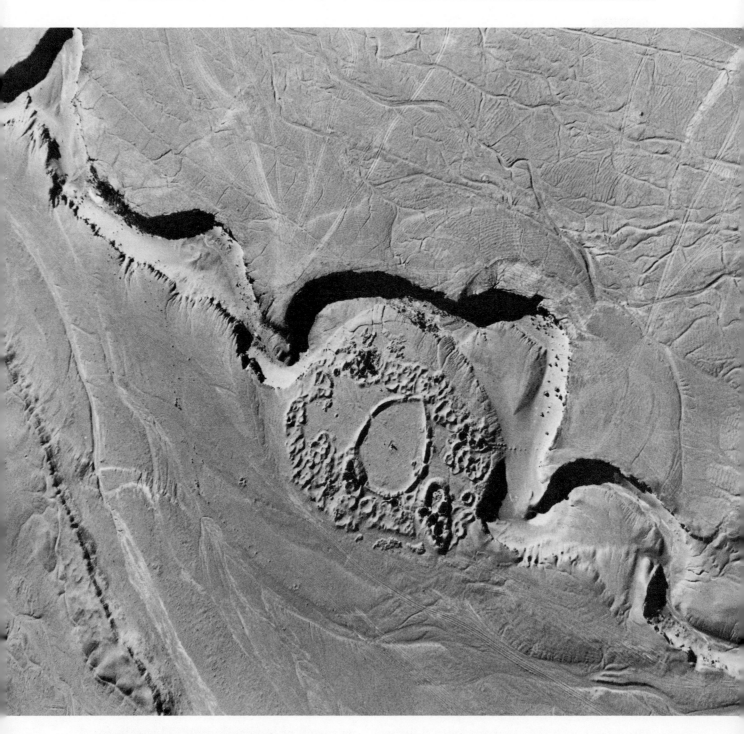

A once-flourishing village depicts the
stark, harsh world of the desert.

for milk. Barter, or exchange of goods, has always been an important aspect of the Wodaabe economy. Besides clothes, the Wodaabe also need cereal and vegetables from the farmers to supplement their milk diet.

Both communities have resisted change, each in its own way. The Aborigines of Jigalong have voluntarily given up their nomadic ways. But they have refused to give up their religion, in spite of pressures to do so. The Wodaabe, on the other hand, stubbornly cling to their nomadic ways. It is possible to explain these differences by looking at how each group views its way of life. The Aborigines did not value their nomadism in itself. It is their religion that gives meaning to their lives. Thus, the Aborigines of Jigalong keep their traditions, and as a result, their identity and pride in themselves.

The Wodaabe, too, are a proud people, intent on keeping their identity. Unlike the Aborigines, however, they consider their nomadism as an act of choice. Their ancestors fled repression in other countries and chose the difficult life of the dry Sahel because they wanted to be free to follow their traditions. The Wodaabe value this freedom. They see any change in their lives as a threat to it. They are suspicious of change. They refer to themselves as "birds in a bush," ready to fly off if anyone comes too close.

Both these communities now face change in their traditional ways. The Aborigines of Jigalong face change because their religion is tied closely to the land and to their nomadic life. Now that they live a settled life away from their homeland, their Law is bound to weaken its hold over them. The Wodaabe face change too, but from the outside. This is because they have begun to use up the resources of the Sahel. They will be forced to develop new ways of adjusting to their environment.

The Great North of Chile is too dry to support human life. Traditionally, people lived in the areas around rivers or other permanent water sources. The rest of the desert remained uninhabited. Chuquicamata and other mining settlements are today located where no food or water is naturally available. These must be brought in, often over great distances. The people of these settlements have succeeded in changing the desert to suit their needs.

Unlike the Wodaabe or the Aborigines of Jigalong, the people of Chuquicamata do not depend directly upon the land for their food or shelter. They are a further step removed from the desert. In return for mining, the people receive money, which they spend for food, shelter, and goods and services.

The people of Chuquicamata, too, face a threat to their life style. They are using up too much water. As a result, the farming communities of the neighborhood are being deprived of their livelihood. The people of Chuquicamata will have to guard against pollution and overuse of their environment or they will be in a difficult situation.

Conserving the desert's resources and maintaining its delicate ecological balance will have to become important considerations in the development of all desert communities.

GLOSSARY

Boomerang—curved club, used as a weapon by Australian Aborigines, that can be thrown so that it will return to the thrower if it misses its target.

Calabash—in Wodaabe society, bowl, bottle, or dipper made by drying and scraping the hard-rinded fruit of the calabash vine. Ceremonial calabashes—made, decorated, and prized by Wodaabe women—are works of art.

Caliche—raw form of sodium nitrate. See *sodium nitrate.*

Cordillera—in Latin America, a system of mountain ranges made up of more than one chain.

Core areas—areas in a region where many objective and subjective elements of culture and environment overlap.

Culture—a way of life devised by people for getting along with the environment and each other.

Decentralization—potential movement of large groups of Australian Aborigines back to their traditional home territories, where they would live in small groups near waterholes.

Dedo—tanned sheepskin decorated with silver studs, worn around the waist by Wodaabe men.

Depot—supply station in Australia.

Desertification—process by which a dry land area is turned into a desert because of climate change or human overuse of the area's vegetation and soil.

Dialects—slightly different variations of a language.

Dreamtime—according to Aborigine beliefs, the period of creation.

Environment—the physical features of the world around us.

Flying Doctor service—in Australia, the name given to the medical service that is provided to distant settlements by means of airplane.

Geothermal—energy created by the heat from the earth.

Gerewol—an annual week-long Wodaabe festival consisting of feasting, dancing, and, especially, a male beauty contest.

Haciendas—plantations or estates in Spanish-speaking America; huge estates concentrated in the central valley of Chile.

Hakkilo—word in Fulfulde, the Wodaabes' language, meaning "care and forethought."

Harmattan—searing desert wind that

blows during the Sahel's dry season. See also *Sahel*.

Hydroelectric power—energy that is created when rushing water pushes huge turbines.

The Law—the basis of all Aborigine beliefs.

Mestizos—in Chilean society, descendants of early Spanish settlers and native Indian women.

Model—a simplification of the real thing.

Munyal—word in Fulfulde, the Wodaabes' language, meaning "patience and fortitude."

Nationalize—to bring industries under government control.

Native Reserve—in Australia, an area where Aborigines can come and go as they please, but which is restricted to outsiders except by permission from the government.

Nomads—people who have no permanent homes; wanderers who move on a regular basis depending on the season.

Oases—natural springs and wells found in arid regions.

Precipitation—water that falls as rain, snow, sleet, or hail.

Pulaku—Fulani code of behavior, which governs how the Wodaabe relate to members of their tribe, their family, and other people.

Region—an area within which elements of culture or environment are similar.

Rotos ("broken ones")—word used to describe Chilean workers who left the security of the hacienda. See also *Haciendas*.

Sahel—semidesert land shared by six West African countries: Mauritania, Senegal, Mali, Bourkina Faso, Niger, and Chad.

Sedentary—living in one place the year round.

Semisedentary—living in one place most of the year.

Semteende—word in Fulfulde, the Wodaabes' language, meaning "reserve and modesty."

Suudu (plural, suudi)—shelter where a Wodaabe wife sleeps, cooks, and keeps her possessions.

Sodium nitrate—mineral salt used as a fertilizer.

Waste smelter heat—heat that escapes from molten metal during processing.

Worso—annual three-day-long Wodaabe festival for celebration of births and marriages.

Wuro—entire Wodaabe homestead, consisting of bed shelters, calf rope, and cattle corral. See also *Suudu*.

FOR
FURTHER
READING

Beckwith, Carol. "Niger's Wodaabe: 'People of the Taboo.' " *National Geographic*, October 1983.

Beckwith, Carol, and van Offelen, Marion. *Nomads of Niger*. New York: Harry N. Abrams, 1983.

George, Jean Craighead. A *Day in the Desert*. New York: Thomas Y. Crowell, 1983.

Merril, Andrea T., ed. *Chile, A Country Study*. Washington, DC: American University Foreign Area Studies, 1982.

Peasley, W. J. *The Last of the Nomads*. Western Australia: Freemantle Arts Centre Press, 1983.

Pond, Alonzo W. *Deserts—Silent Lands of the World*. New York: W. W. Norton and Co., Inc., 1965.

Robinson, Roland Edward. *The Australian Aboriginal*. London: A. H. & A. W. Reed Pty. Ltd., 1977.

Rudolph, William E. *Vanishing Trails of Atacama*. New York: American Geographical Society, 1963.

Tonkinson, Robert. *The Jigalong Mob: Aboriginal Victors of the Desert Crusade*. Menlo Park, California: Cummings Publishing Co., 1974.

————. *The Mardudjara Aborigines: Living the Dream in Australia's Desert*. New York: Holt, Rinehart and Winston, 1978.

INDEX

Aborigines, 46–62
    celebrations of, 46, 52, 53
    future of, 58, 62
    houses of, 55, 56
    in Jigalong, 54, 56–58, 62, 85
    nomadic life of, 46, 83, 85
    paintings of, 51
    religion of, 50–52, 85
Africa. *See* Salel region; Wodaabe
Allende Gossins, Salvador, 72, 75
American Indians, 52
Antofagasta, 77
Australia. *See* Aborigines; Western Desert

Biosphere, 14
Boomerangs, 46
Bourkina Faso, 21

Calabashes, 29, 31
Caliche, 65
Carnegie, David, 45–46
Cattle, 13, 14, 29, 31, 32, 38–39, 41
Celebrations:
    Aboriginal, 46, 52, 53
    Wodaabe, 36, 38
Chad, 21
Children, Wodaabe, 35, 36, 39
Chile, 65–79, 85
    farming in, 18, 72
    rainfall in, 17–18
    religion in, 68
    society in, 68
    See also Chuquicamata

Chileanization, 75
Chiu Chiu, 72
Chuquicamata, 13, 83, 85
    history of, 72, 75
    life in, 69, 72
    people of, 75–76, 79
Climate:
    in Norte Grande, 65
    in Sahel, 18, 21
    in Western Desert, 13, 45
    See also Rainfall
Clothing, 13
    Wodaabe, 35, 83
CODELCO, 75
Copper, 13, 14, 65, 69–72, 75–76
Cordillera, 65
Core areas, 15, 17
Corroborees, 53
Cultural geography:
    defined, 14
    study of regions, 15–17
Culture, 13
    defined, 14
    interaction with environment, 17–18

Darwin, Charles, 65
Decentralization, 58
Dedo, 35
Depot, 54
Desertification, 39, 41
Dialects, 56
Dreamtime, 50–52
Drought, 14, 18, 21, 23, 35, 39, 41

Environment:
    defined, 14
    interaction with culture, 17–18

Farming:
    in Chile, 18, 72
    in Sahel, 27
Flying Doctor service, 56
Flying foxes, 49
Forrest, John, 45
Fulani code, 36
Fulanis, 26, 27
Fulfulde, 27

Geothermal energy, 72
Gerewol, 36, 38
Gibson Desert, Australia, 45–46
Great North Desert. *See* Norte Grande
Great Sandy Desert, Australia, 45
Great Victoria Desert, Australia, 45

Haciendas, 68, 75
Hakkilo, 36
Harmattan, 21
Homes:
    Aborigine, 55, 56
    in Chuquicamata, 69
    Wodaabe, 23, 29, 31
Hydroelectric power, 72

Irrigation, 18
Islam, 27

Jigalong, Australia, 13, 54, 56–58, 62, 85
Jigalong Mob, The: Aboriginal Victors of the Desert Crusade (Tonkinson), 54

Law, the, 50, 52, 57, 85
Literacy, 68

Mali, 21

Marriage, Wodaabe, 27, 32, 35, 36
Mauritania, 21, 23
Mestizos, 68
Millet, 26, 32
Mining:
    in Chile, 13, 65, 68–72, 75–76
    in Jigalong, 58
Munyal, 36

Nationalization, 75
Native Reserve, 54
Niger, 21, 27
Nitrate, 69, 75
Nomadic life:
    of Aborigines, 46, 83, 85
    of Wodaabe, 21, 23, 27, 28, 38, 83, 85
Norte Grande (Great Northern Desert), Chile, 65–79, 85
    climate and rainfall in, 65
    See also Chile; Chuquicamata
Northern Territory, 58

Oases, 27
Overgrazing, 41

Paintings, Aborigine, 50
Pinochet Ugarte, Augusto, 75
Population density, 13, 21, 65
Precipitation. *See* Rainfall
Pulaku, 36

Rainfall, 13–15
    in Norte Grande, 65
    in Sahel, 18, 21, 22, 32
    in Western Desert, 45
Ranching, 41
Refugee camps, in Sahel, 39, 41
Regions, 15, 17
Religion:
    Aborigine, 50–52, 85
    in Chile, 68

Sahara Desert, 39
Sahel region, Africa, 13
    climate and rainfall in, 18, 21, 22,
       32
    drought in, 14, 18, 21, 35, 39, 41
    farming in, 27
    refugee camps in, 39, 41
    See also Wodaabe
San Pero de Atacama, 72
Sedentary existence, 27
Semisedentary existence, 27
Semteende, 36
Senegal, 21
Sodium nitrate, 65
Soil erosion, 39
Solar energy, 72
Songs, Aborigine, 51–52
Squatters, 79
Storytelling, 36
Strikes, 75–76
Suudi, 29, 31

Tonkinson, Robert, 54
Transportation, 14, 21, 69
Tuaregs, 27

Unions, 75–76

Vegetation, 13, 15, 16, 45, 47

Waste smelter heat, 72
Water, 13, 18, 72, 74, 85
Western Desert, Australia:
    climate and rainfall in, 13, 45
    See also Aborigines
Wodaabe, 13, 21–41
    celebrations of, 36, 38
    change and, 38–39, 41
    clothing of, 35, 83
    homes of, 23, 29, 31
    marriage, 27, 32, 35, 36
    nomadic life of, 21, 23, 27, 28, 38, 83,
      85
    origins of, 27
    work, 31–32, 35
Women:
    Aborigine, 46, 52
    in Chile, 79
    Wodaabe, 29, 31, 32
Worso, 36
Wuro, 31

ABOUT
THE AUTHOR

Nayana Currimbhoy grew up in Bombay, India, and completed her education in the United States. She now lives in New York City, where she works as a freelance writer. Besides writing books for young adults, Currimbhoy is an editor at *Interiors* magazine and is currently working on a novel.